D0090702

DOES YOUR HOUSE HAVE LIONS?

Sonia

DOES YOUR HOUSE HAVE LIONS?

Sanchez

BEACON PRESS

BOSTON

BEACON PRESS
25 Beacon Street
Boston, Massachusetts 02108-2892

BEACON PRESS BOOKS
are published under the auspices of
the Unitarian Universalist Association of Congregations.

"sister's voice" was previously published in *PSA News,* volume 43,
newsletter of the Poetry Society of America, winter 1994.

© 1997 by Sonia Sanchez
All rights reserved
Printed in the United States of America

01 00 99 98 97   8 7 6 5 4 3 2

Text design by Elizabeth Elsas

LIBRARY OF CONGRESS CATALOGING-IN-PUBLICATION DATA
Sanchez, Sonia, 1935–
        Does your house have lions? / Sonia Sanchez.
            p.   cm.
        ISBN 0-8070-6830-6 (cloth)
        1. Afro-Americans—Poetry.   I. Title
    PS3569.A468D64   1997
    811´.54—dc21   96-44574

811.54
SAN
1997

to Barbara who shared her family and
Orcas Island with me and
to all my sisters who have lost their brothers to AIDS.

One day in the late sixties, I was on the phone with Rahsaan and mentioned to him that just that day I had bought a house. He responded by asking, "Does your house have lions?" I said, "What?" He said, "Lions. You know, like in front of a museum or the post office. You know, concrete lions. My house has lions. Get a house with lions."

JOEL DORN
May 1993

from the *Rahsaan Roland Kirk Anthology*

Contents

sister's

voice

this was a migration unlike
the 1900s of black men and women
coming north for jobs. freedom. life.
this was a migration to begin
to bend a father's heart again
to birth seduction from the past
to repay desertion at last.

imagine him short and black
thin mustache draping thin lips
imagine him country and exact
thin body, underfed hips
watching at this corral of battleships
and bastards. watching for forget
and remember. dancing his pirouette.

and he came my brother at seventeen
recruited by birthright and smell
grabbing the city by the root with clean
metallic teeth. commandant and infidel
pirating his family in their cell
and we waited for the anger to retreat
and we watched him embrace the city and the street.

first he auctioned off his legs. eyes.
heart. in rooms of specific pain.
he specialized in generalize
learned newyorkese and all profane.
enslaved his body to cocaine
denied his father's signature
damned his sister's overture.

and a new geography greeted him.
the atlantic drifted from offshore
to lick his wounds to give him slim
transfusion as he turned changed wore
a new waistcoat of solicitor
antidote to his southern skin
ammunition for a young paladin.

and the bars. the glitter. the light
discharging pain from his bygone anguish
of young black boy scared of the night.
sequestered on this new bank, he surveyed the fish
sweet cargoes crowded with scales feverish
with quick sales full sails of flesh
searing the coastline of his acquiesce.

and the days rummaging his eyes
and the nights flickering through a slit
of narrow bars. hips. thighs.
and his thoughts labeling him misfit
as he prowled, pranced in the starlit
city, coloring his days and nights
with gluttony and praise and unreconciled rites.

brother's

voice

father. i despise you for abandoning me
to aunts and mothers and ministers of tissue
tongues, nibbling at my boyish knee.
father. forgive me for i know not what they do
moving me backwards through seams of bamboo
masks, staring eyes campaigning for
my attention. come O lords; my extended metaphor.

sister. i am not your true brother
one half of me resides in my mother's breast
in her eyes where tears exceed their worth.
the other half walks on tiptoe to divest
his tongue of me, this father always a guest
never a permanent resident of my veins
always a traveler to other terrains.

mother. i love you. you are my living saint
walking inside my skull you multiply out loud
in dainty dreams seraphim smiles without a tint
of mystery. you move among us with dark
gait intrepid steps that disavowed
retirement from an elaborate sex
while you prepared each morning's text.

the sermon for each day was my father
husband who left you shipwrecked with child
the movie of the week was my father
staring out from philco screens while your wild
dreams of nouveau lady genuflecting in single file
in a southern city of mouths on mascaraed thighs
twentieth century of elasticized lies.

what does a liver know of peace
or spleen. kidneys. ribs. be still my soul.
how does a city broker its disease
within the confines of a borough, where control
limps tepid—like carrying a parasol
of hurts, hurting, hurted, hurtful croons
stranded in measured arenas without pulpits or spittoons.

came the summer of nineteen sixty
harlem luxuriating in Malcolm's voice
became Big Red beautiful became a city
of magnificent Black Birds steel eyes moist
as he insinuated his words of sweet choice
while politicians complained about this racist
this alchemist. this strategist. this purist.

came the rallies sponsored by new york core
came Malcolm with speeches spilling exact and compact
became a traveling man who revived the poor
who answered with slow echoes became cataract
and fiesta became future and flashback
filling the selves with an old outrage
piercing the cold corners with a new carriage.

ALBUQUERQUE ACADEMY LIBRARY

then i began an awakening a flowering outside
the living dead became a wanderer of air
barking at the stars became a bride
bridegroom of change timeless black with hair
moist with kinks and morning dare
then i began to think me alive with form and history
then i made my former life an accessory.

how to erect respect in a country of men
where dollars pump their veins?
how to return from exile from swollen
tongues crisscrossing my frail domain?
how to learn to love me amid all the pain?
how to look into his eyes and be reborn
without blood and phlegm and thorn?

father's

voice

the day he traveled to my daughter's house
it was june. he cursed me with his morning nod
of anger as he filtered his callous
walk. skip. hop. feet slipshod
from 125th street bars, face curled with odd
reflections. the skin of a father is accented
in the sentence of the unaccented.

i was a southern Negro man playing music
married to a high yellow woman who loved my unheard
face, who slept with me in nordic
beauty. i prisoner since my birth to fear
i unfashioned buried in an open grave
of mornings unclapped with constant sight
of masters fattened decked with my diminished light.

this love. this first wife of mine, died in childbirth
this face of complex lace exiled her breath
into another design, and i died became wanderlust
demanded recompense from friends for my heartbreak
cursed the land for this new heartache
put her away with a youthful pause
never called her name again, wrapped my heart in gauze.

became romeo bound, applauded women
as i squeezed their syrup, drank their stenciled
face, danced between their legs, placed my swollen
shank to the world, became man distilled
early twentieth-century black man fossilled
fulfilled by women things, foreclosing on my life.
mother where do i go before i arrive?

she wasn't as beautiful as my first wife
this ruby-colored girl insinuating her limb
against my thigh positioning her wild-life
her non-virginal smell as virginal her climb
towards me with slow walking heels made me limp
made me stumble, made my legs squint
until i stopped, stepped inside her footprint.

i did not want to leave you son, this flame
this pecan-colored festival requested me
not my child, your sister. your mother could not frame
herself as her mother and i absentee
father, and i nightclub owner carefree
did not heed her blood, did not see my girl's eyes
shaved buckled down with southern thighs.

now my seventy-eight years urge me on your land
now my predator legs prey, broadcast
no new nightmares no longer birdman
of cornerstone comes, i come to collapse the past
while bonfires burn up your orphan's mask
i sing a dirge of lost black southern manhood
this harlem man begging pardon, secreting old.

i was told i don't remember who
i think i was told he entered his sister's house
cursed me anew, tried to tattoo
her tongue with worms, tried to arouse
her slumbering veins to espouse
his venom and she leaned slapped him still
stilled his mouth across early morning chill.

rumor has it that he slapped her hard
down purgatorial sounds of caress
rumor has it that he rushed her down a boulevard
of mad laughter while his hands grabbed harness—
like her arms and she, avenger and she heiress
to naked lightning, detonated him, began her dance
of looted hems gathering together for his inheritance.

blood the sound of blood paddling down the road
blood the taste of blood choking their eyes
and my son's body blood-stained red
with country-lies, city-lies, father-lies, mother-lies,
and my daughter clamoring to exorcise
old thieves trespassing in an old refrain
conjured up a blue-black chord to ordain.

wa ma ne ho mene so oo
oseee yei, oseee yei, oseee yei
wa ma ne ho mene so oo
he has become holy as he walks toward daresay
can you hear his blood tissue ready to pray
he who wore death discourages any plague
he who was an orphan now recollects his legs.

wa ma ne ho mene so oo: he is arising in all his majesty
oseee yei: a shout of praise

family

voices

———

ancestors'

voices

brother's voice

there is nothing i do not comprehend
i have become a collector of shouts
hold my ears father, i have come to mend
our hearts raise a glass celebrate root out
lyrical slaughters become your only son devout
i have become a lover of sweet water
i worship stone i will not betray you father.

father's voice

steady your hand old man do not trouble
yourself with language, stalk his wound
he is listening to your corpuscles cradle
the clap and thunder of a new sound
he has called your name and old teeth are found
can you hold me son, as i rise from this whimper
can you hear me son, as i cross over this river.

father's voice

i am preparing for his coming, i sit on my flesh
i am wealthy my limbs free of moths
i am in praise of convalesce
i will stand free of the walking sabbaths
i will return sermons crowded with cloths
i am learning how to talk to my son's dust
i have tossed my net toward a future trust.

ancestor's voice (male)

do you remember me,	huh?
when our teeth were iron,	huh?
did you drum about me,	hey?
and not babylon,	hey?
did you take your weapon,	huh?
rattle it on any mattress,	hey?
til you became powerless?	hey, huh, heyyyyyyyy?

ancestor's voice (female)

do you remember me,	ayyyyyy?
when our wombs were cerebral,	ayyyyyy?
did you dream about me,	ayyyyyy?
and not betrayal,	ayyyyyy?
did you take your coastal	
blood to any playground	ayyyyyy?
to every resident clown?	ayyyyyyyyyyyy?

sister's voice

let the spirit raise up echoes in my spine
brother. let our histories bleed no boomerangs
let my accent shrink the itch of undermine
brother. let our mouths speak without harangue
let my journey sing a path they sang
O i will purchase my brother's whisper.
O i will reward my brother's tongue.

ancestor's voice (female)

have you prepared a place of honor for me?
have you recalled us from death?
where is the *mmenson* to state our history?
where are the griots the food my failed breath?
where is the morning path i crossed in good faith?
what terror slows your journey to this dawn?
have you prepared a place for us to mourn?

mmenson: orchestra of seven elephant tusk horns used on state occasions to
relate history

ancestor's voice (male)

water from my feet i return to you
oceans from my eyes to drown your bones
i am turning my heart away from you
hundreds of years have passed with no memorial stones
how can i forgive myself without the ritual horns?
your stool sits too long at this testimony
your stool forgets the flesh of ceremony.

brother's voice

i travel to India, father, Sai Baba says i must return
home seeking the light of the soft stone smile
i travel to India, father, Sai Baba says my turn
has come to prostrate pray reconcile
my soul with him who enters single file
i worship the light of the timid ground
i walk wide-eyed through blue slits of sound.

brother's voice

sister tell me about this marriage crown
you wear, tell me how to claim it all without fanfare
i want children, dreamers of the upside down
i want children screamers with kinky hair
i want a rocking chair child for my heir.
sister i want my tongue curling forward with this
while my face flows full with promise.

brother's voice

sister tell me about this cough i cough
all of my skin cradled in this cough
my body ancient as this white cough, i cough
all day and night i'm haunted by this cough,
a snake rattles in my throat this cough, i cough
a scream embalms my chest with cough
sister an echo surrounds my lungs with this cough, i cough.

brother's voice

i linger in stethoscopes and thermometers at Lenox Hill
i have entered the hospital to test
the cough and temperature making me ill
i have entered this hospital to rest
and all i have discovered is unrest
the doctor says happily it is not pneumonia or cancer
the doctor says my temperature is like a trickster.

ancestor's voice (male)

it is necessary to remember the sea
never forget how it leaps out of nowhere
it is necessary to remember the sea
holding your ancestors in a nightmare
of waves smooth breasts of warfare
is there no anguish no balm of Gilead for the dead?
is there no amulet for this coming dread?

ancestor's voice (female)

why won't you stand up
show us how to dare
why won't you stand up
investigate this nightmare
show us how to prepare
your children's eyes stand at attention
your children's eyes itch for resurrection.

ancestor's voice (female)

drink this tea
(bitter-heyyyyyy?) as bitter
as my bones hugging the sea
pour salt into the laughter
of eyes popping out of water
tears sail down my one eye
ornamental anger parts my smile.

sister's voice

come down to my house in philadelphia man
what you need is a cleansing of the body
come down to philadelphia where i can fan
your blood cool take custody
of your infection flood it into frailty
come down and i will defend your skin
against the threat of constant confession.

brother's voice

i checked myself out of the hospital
sister. i'm back at work on a new skyscraper
i'm piecing together the city in a recital
of steel and windows. no rice paper
walls here to destroy my design. no bootlegger
wires light this expensive east-side dwelling
up here, my limbs sequester themselves in lightning

father's voice

i'm leaving this message on your voice mail
your brother's back in the hospital temperature 105
i've called his mother, she arrives tomorrow wholesale
the doctors wait for me at every corner they arrive
with stationary voices tracking the sweat-hive
of his body embroidering needles on his veins
i pray his corpuscles learn how to abstain.

father's voice

where to go?
where to go today?
where to have gone at some ago
time when he was at play
in the world? what kind of day
is this where a son's body bleeds feces?
what kind of day anoints his flesh with effigies?

ancestor's voice (female)

i hear the water whistling in squads
of blue comings, the ocean has become a thief
i see our souls transported, lightning rods
of apocalyptic disbelief
the sea opens and shuts with our grief
new fathers have come to record their loss
old fathers know this accustomed chaos.

mother's voice

i am here my baby in your hospital room
i am here my love i have kissed your morning breath
i have walked around your father's gloom
i have come straight to see you grazing near death
you are hot at the edge of this city's wealth
the doctors praise your courage your ancestral smell
the doctors record your body's constant betrayal.

mother's voice

i have waited all day for this stepdaughter
i have made a special time for her voice
she is late, talking on her own to another doctor
i must prepare my tongue for the proper choice
of words, make my eyes full, moist.
i will let them operate on his diminished body
i will indulge their hands in this new fantasy.

daughter's voice

mothermothermother
dead when i was one
stepmotherstepmotherstepmother
alive with overdone
let his final days be a monotone
no cuttings no more stabbings of arms and legs
no resident tubes to collect these final dregs.

brother's voice

O forgive me mother
O forgive me father
O forgive me sister
O forgive me fever
O forgive me tremor
O forgive me rumor
O forgive me terror.

brother's voice

dress me in white
not hospital white
dress me in white
of my ancestor's white
of Sai Baba's white
of my morning white
of my spirit's white.

brother's voice

i am going out of my cell
i am ready
ring the bell (3 times)
i am ready
I have fitted my legs with mercy
my eyes say no requiem
mangi dem, mangi dem, mangi dem

mangi dem: goodbye (i am going)

brother's voice

hold me with air
breathe me with air
sponge me with air
whisper me with air
comb me with air
brush me with air
rinse me with air.

brother's voice

i come. doctor.
mangi nyo. captor.
i come. inventor.
mangi nyo. censor.
i come. preacher.
mangi nyo. confessor.
i come. ancestor.

mangi nyo: i come

ancestor's voice

FEMALE *jamma ga fanan*

MALE look at his eyes. is he Asian?

FEMALE *jamma ga fanan*

MALE look at his hair. is he Indian?

FEMALE *jamma ga fanan*

MALE look at his cheekbones. is he Native American?

FEMALE *jamma ga fanan*

MALE look at his hands. is he African American?

jamma ga fanan: good morning

ancestor's voice

FEMALE   *nyata?* how much is this death rattle?

MALE   *nyata?* he is not owned by anyone here or there.

FEMALE   *nyata?* how much for this bundle of applause circling his everywhere?

MALE   *nyata?* how much for the walking air?

FEMALE   *nyata?* how much for him to share this blue ash?

MALE   *nyata?* how much for him to share the calabash?

nyata: how much

ancestor's voice

FEMALE where are the gods when we need them?

MALE they are stammering someplace off camera.

FEMALE where are their masks, their substitute emblem?

MALE they rustle in weeds like an old dilemma.

FEMALE where is Buddha? Allah? Jehovah? Ptah? Ra?

MALE will their tongues acknowledge us one day?

FEMALE will their cobwebs remember us one day?

ancestor's voice (family)

TO BE SUNG

MALE	*sala maleikum*	hello
FEMALE	*nanga def*	how are you?
MALE	*sala maleikum*	hello
BROTHER	*magni fi rek*	i am well
BROTHER	*dama buga lek*	i want to eat
BROTHER	*dama buga naan*	i want to drink
MALE/FEMALE	*kai fi African*	come here African
MALE/FEMALE	*kai fi African*	come here African
BROTHER	*mangi nyo*	i am coming
BROTHER	*mangi nyo*	i am coming
BROTHER	*mangi nyo*	i am coming . . .